Handbook of
Sitar

HISTORY | ANATOMY | TUNING | MAINTENANCE

Handbook of Sitar

HISTORY | ANATOMY | TUNING | MAINTENANCE

Author
Pankaj Vishal

Pankaj Publications
New Delhi, INDIA

Pankaj's Handbook of Sitar
First Published May, 2008
Copyright © Pankaj Publications

ISBN 13 :978-81-87155-95-9
ISBN 10 :81-87155-95-7

Published by :
PANKAJ PUBLICATION
M-114, Vikas Puri
New Delhi 110 018
Email : contact@pankajmusic.com
www.pankajmusic.com

For bulk purchases and business inquiries,
contact@pankajmusic.com

DISCLAIMER

This book is being sold/distributed subject to the exclusive condition that neither the author nor the publishers, individually or collectively, shall be responsible to indemnify the buyer/user/possessor of this book beyond the selling price of this book for any circumstances. If not agreed, please do not buy/accept/use/possess this book.

- *publishers*

Cover design by	:	Square vision
Typesetting by	:	Reliable Infomedia
Illustrations by	:	Reliable Infomedia & Mohit Suneja

All rights reserved. This work is the author's own tested work, and he has right to recognise any violations made to this copy. No part of this book may be reproduced, stored in a retrieval system or transmitted in any form or by any means electronic, mechanical, photocopying recording or otherwise, without prior written permission of the publisher.

Preface

Music is considered to have a divine origin and one which brings its practitioner very close to God. It is said that God created music to give a proof of His presence. Therefore, the existence of music is as old as humanity itself. But later it came to be presumed that music is an inborn quality, given by God Himself, and therefore it can not be learned here on this earth. One may be trained in music and excel, provided there is genetic support. But, it is not a universal fact. One can learn everything with proper sincerity and devotion.

Keeping this in view, the present series of hand books has been prepared as a reference material for those who have just got in a formal touch with music and if it knocks the gate of anyone's emotional energy, to proceed further in this field. For this, we have selected one of the oldest instruments of our music tradition - the Sitar. It is an instrument which is capable of energizing anyone's senses with its sweet sound.

Moreover, our classical instrumental music has an edge over other forms of music of the world. Vocal music has a sort of limitation as it is bound in words, hence it leaves the audience with a limited scope of imagination, largely confined to the meaning of words and its ambience. But contrary to that, an instrument communicates with the audience in an affective form and energizes the senses according to the imagination of an individual listener. It does not confine the listener to any area and thus leaves with enormous possibilities of imagination. That is why a book in the form of a handbook has been brought out to facilitate a beginner in familiarizing himself with the so called difficulties of Sitar, so that if one feels the necessities for enjoying instrumental music, he may have a ready reference at the initial stage itself.

This book does not claim to give you details and intricacies of music as well as of Sitar but it will, most certainly, give you a plain to stand on. Moreover, this book does not intend to replace the position of a guru in the field of music. The principal aim of this book is to provide a ready reckoner to the beginners for satiating all inquisitiveness related to music in general and the Sitar in particular.

I would like to place on record the blessings of my revered guru, Sarod maestro, Pt. Sunil Mukherjee, whose teaching and training has enabled me to understand the nuances of music such as its philosophical as well as emotional aspects. I am also indebted to my first guru, Pt. Mor Mukut Kedia, who made me capable of holding the Sitar and write this book.

I am also indebted to my parents, who, in spite of all odds in life, did not discourage me but gave all their support to pursue music.

The publisher of this book, Mr Vikas Bajaj, and the publishing house - PANKAJ PUBLICATION, deserve special mention and thanks for carrying out this enormous job which is in fact a small step towards saving this old and dying tradition of our Indian culture.

Any suggestion to enhance the quality of this book is heartedly solicited.

- PANKAJ VISHAL

Contents

Preface... v

Part 1: Theory of Music — 9-40
The Indian Music System — 11
Lay (Tempo or Speed) — 21
Taal (The Rhythm) — 24
Indian Music Notation System — 30
Format of Music on Sitar — 32
Western Notation System — 34
Points to remember in Combined Notation System — 39

Part 2: The Sitar - Then & Now — 41-54
History and Development — 43
Indian String Instruments — 46
Famous Sitarists — 50

Part 3: Know The Sitar — 55-66
Various Types of Sitar — 57
Parts of a Sitar — 60
Strings & Frets — 65

Part 4: Playing The Sitar — 67-72
Sitting Positions — 69
Important Tips While Playing the Sitar — 71

Part 5: Sounds and Notes — 73-82

Production of Basic Bols — 75
Position of Notes on Frets — 78
Steps to Shift the Frets — 79
Playing Basic Swaras — 80

Part 6: Tuning and Maintenance of a Sitar — 83-92

Tuning the Sitar — 85
Repairs & Maintenance of a Sitar — 90
Tips for Buying a Sitar — 92

Part - 1
Theory of Music

The Indian Music System

Indian Music is based on *Ragas* and *Ragas* are based on the *Nadas, Shrutis, Swaras, Saptaka* and *Thaats*, as shown in the evolution chart.

Nada (Sound) : This is sound produced by striking, friction or beating. 'Nada' is of two kinds:

(a) *Sangeet-un-upyogi Nada* **(Non-Musical sound)**: Those sounds which are not musical such as machine rattlings, traffic horns, shouting etc. These sounds are not pleasant to listen to and are disturbing in nature. They can cause headaches and irritation. We hear these sounds in our day-to-day lives in the city.

(b) *Sangeet-upyogi Nada* **(Musical sound):** Contrary to non-musical sounds, these sounds are pleasant to listen to and musically audible. These can be the sounds of nature as the chirping of birds, water falls, flowing river, singing etc. These sounds are relaxing and give a feeling of tranquility and peace. Musical sounds like singing and instrumental playing have the virtue to hypnotize an audience.

Shruti **(Microtonal Interval notes)**: These are microtonal sounds found between **Sangeet-upyogi Nadas** (musical sounds). They can be heard and distinguished by a sensitive musical ear only. They can now be seen visually on an 'Oscilloscope'. *Shrutis* are also called Microtonal Intervals of Sound. The gaps are increased between the sounds to make these **Shrutis** to **notes** for the purpose of easy recognition and the development of music by using them when playing and singing.

There are 22 *Shrutis* used in Indian Music.

1. Tivra	8. Raudri	15. Rakta
2. Kumudwati	9. Krodhi	16. Sandipini
3. Manda	10. Vajrika	17. Alapini
4. Chhandovati	11. Prasarini	18. Madanti
5. Dayawati	12. Priti	19. Rohini
6. Ranjani	13. Manjari	20. Romya
7. Raktika	14. Kshiti	21. Ugra
		22. Kshobhini

Swaras (Notes): *Swaras* (notes) are produced by *Shrutis* with big intervals or Gaps. They can be distinguished by the ears of listeners. The difference between '*Swaras*' and '*Shrutis*' is that the '*Swaras*' are measured by *Shrutis* depending on the intervals or number of *Shrutis*.

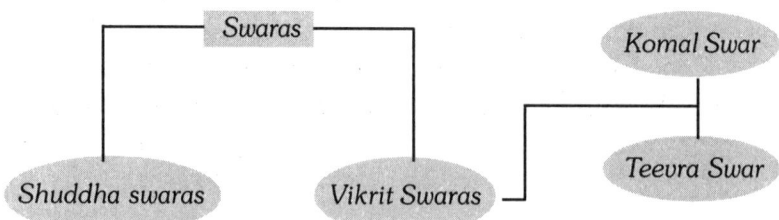

*Swara*s are of two types, *Vikrits* **Swara (Distorted note)** and **Shuddha Swara (Full Tone note)**

Shuddha Swaras (Full Tone Notes). These are natural notes which are found in the *Shrutis*. To recognize the minute gap of *Shrutis* easily.

Shudha Swaras or Full Tone Notes were identified and called **Natural notes** and they are 7 of them.

Vedic names along with the popular short names of these 7 notes are given below. The complete music theory is based on these 7 notes and their combinations.

S. No.	Name of Swaras	Shuddha Swaras	Western Notes	Shruti
1.	Shadaj	Sa	C	4 Tivra, Kumudwati, Manda Chhandovati.
2.	Rishabh	Re	D	3 Dayawati, Ranjani, Raktika
3.	Gandhar	Ga	E	2 Raudri & Krodhi
4.	Madhyam	Ma	F	4 Vajrika, Prasarini, Priti, Manjari
5.	Pancham	Pa	G	4 Kshiti, Rakta, Sandipini Alapini
6.	Dhaiwat	Dha	A	3 Madanti, Rohini, Romya
7.	Nishad	Ni	B	2 Ugra Kshobhini

With the identification of these full tone notes the gap between the notes becomes wider. The wider the gap the greater the obstruction to the sweetness of sound. Musicians then introduced **Half Tone Notes** or **Flat Notes** (*Komal Swaras*) between two **Full Tone Notes** (*Shuddha Swaras*), and thus **Distorted notes** (*Vikrit Swaras*) came into existance.

Vikrit Swaras **(Distorted Notes)** : *Vikrit Swara*s are of two types, they are *Komal Swara*s (Flat Notes or Half Tone Notes) and *Tivra Swara* (Sharp note). With the introduction of the distorted notes, *Sa* and *Pa* though remained unchanged.

Komal Swaras **(Flat notes or Half Tone Notes)** are found between two **shudha swaras (Full Tone notes)**. These *Swara*s are a bit lower in pitch from the *Shuddha Swara*s. They are symbolized in notation by a Dash (_) below the note such as **Re**. A half step lower.

✌ There are four *Komal Swara*s (flat notes). These are: **Re, Ga, Dha, & Ni.**

Tivra Swar is the note which appears a half step above the full note and is called a **sharp note (*Tivra Swar*)**. This *Swar* (note) is higher in pitch from the *Shuddha Swara*. It is symbolized in notation by a small vertical line (') over the note.

✌ There is only one *Tivra Swar*, which is **Ma'**.

According to two different notation systems, it is important to understand the difference between the two. There are two fixed notes in Indian system. These are **Sa & Pa**. The remaining five notes have two different types as semitone or distorted forms. On the other hand there are two types for all the seven notes in the western system. There is a distortion of each note and all the notes can be either flat or sharp. The closest related western note to the Indian distorted notes are as follows -

Indian Notes	Re	Ga	Ma'	Dha	Ni
Western Notes	C# or D♭	D# or E♭	F# or G♭	G# or A♭	A# or B♭

1. As shown in the table, note *komal* **Re** is shown as it is but in western system, it is written as two types, either **C#** or **D♭**. Where (#) symbol is used for sharp (*tivra*) and (♭) symbol is used for flat (*komal*).

2. There are two fixed notes in the Indian system. These are **Sa** & **Pa**, which cannot be changed to flats or sharp.

3. Western music does not have sharp for note **E** & **B**. Instead, **F** stands for **E#**, and **C** stands for **B#**.

This is how the Twelve notes come to exist. They are as follows.

Sl. No.	Swaras	Description	Western Name
1.	**Sa**	*Shudha* (Fixed)	**C Fixed**
2.	Re	*Komal*	D Half Tone note
3.	**Re**	*Shuddha*	**D Full tone note**
4.	Ga	*Komal*	E Half tone note
5.	**Ga**	*Shuddha*	**E Full tone note**
6.	**Ma**	*Shudha*	**F Full tone note**
7.	Ma'	*Tivra*	F Sharp note
8.	**Pa**	*Shuddha* (Fixed)	**G Fixed**
9.	Dha	*Komal*	A Half tone note
10.	**Dha**	*Shuddha*	**A Full note**
11.	Ni	*Komal*	B Half Tone note
12.	**Ni**	*Shuddha*	**B Full Note**

A group of these 7 Natural Notes (*Shuddha Swaras*) make a *Saptak* (Octave). The *Saptak* also includes 4 *Komal* and one *Tivra Swar*. In all there are 12 Notes to make a complete **Saptak (Octave).** A *Saptak* (Octave) includes the *guru* notes of Indian Music which are **Sa Re Ga Ma Pa Dha Ni.** A specific combination of these *Swara*s (Notes) from the *Saptak* forms a **Thaat (scale)**, which is the basis of the *Ragas*.

Ragas (Melodies) are a particular combination of these notes or group of notes, which are produced from **Thaats (scales)**.

In a nutshell, we can understand the journey of swaras from its origin to Nada by this evolution chart.

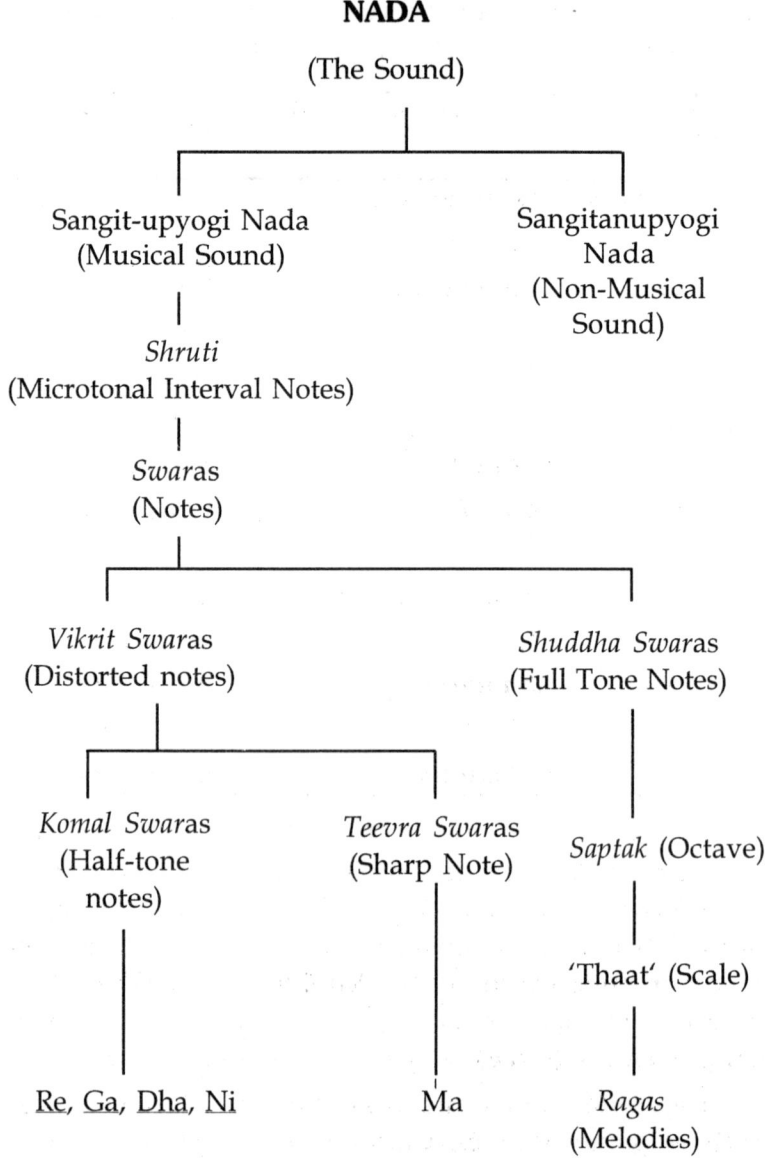

SAPTAK (Octave)

According to the Indian theory of music there are three ranges of the human voice, which are low, medium and high pitch. These pitches when identified with notes in music called *Saptaka* or a group of seven *Shuddha* notes. These seven notes also includes four *komal* and one *Tivra Swara*. The human voice is differentiated under these three ranges:

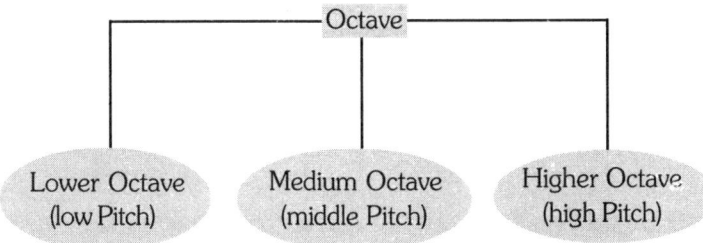

1. **Madhya Saptaka** (Medium Octave) — When the sound naturally comes out of the throat without any pressure, it is called the throat voice. The Medium octave or *Madhya Saptaka*.

2. **Mandra Saptaka** (Lower Octave) — When the sound comes out entirely by the pressure of the lungs, it is called the chest voice or *Mandra Saptaka* (Lower Octave). In this *Saptaka* the pitch of the sound is lower than the medium octave.

3. **Tar Saptaka** (Upper Octave) — When the sound is produced with the exertion of force on the nostrils and head, called the head voice or *Tar Saptaka* (Upper Octave). The pitch or sound is higher than that of the medium octave.

THAAT

Ordinarily a *Thaat* is a combination of **seven Swaras** or notes capable of producing *Ragas*. All the notes played in *thaat* are in ascending order starting from **Sa** ending at **Ni,** whether natural, flat or sharp. There are basically ten *thaats* in Indian music system.

The *Thaat* must qualify these three Basic conditions :

1. A *Thaat* must contain the seven *swaras* (notes) in the regular form.

2. The *Shuddha, Komal* or *Tivra Swaras* must appear one after the other.

3. It is a mere scale, a combination of notes. It does not essentially need to please the listeners ear.

Ten thaats and their notes as follows:

1.	Bilawal	Sa	Re	Ga	Ma	Pa	Dha	Ni
2.	Khamaj	Sa	Re	Ga	Ma	Pa	Dha	<u>Ni</u>
3.	Kafee	Sa	Re	<u>Ga</u>	Ma	Pa	Dha	<u>Ni</u>
4.	Asawari	Sa	Re	<u>Ga</u>	Ma	Pa	<u>Dha</u>	<u>Ni</u>
5.	Bhairav	Sa	<u>Re</u>	Ga	Ma	Pa	<u>Dha</u>	Ni
6.	Kalyan	Sa	Re	Ga	Ma'	Pa	Dha	Ni
7.	Poorvi	Sa	<u>Re</u>	Ga	Ma	Pa	<u>Dha</u>	Ni
8.	Bhairavi	Sa	<u>Re</u>	<u>Ga</u>	Ma	Pa	<u>Dha</u>	<u>Ni</u>
9.	Todi	Sa	<u>Re</u>	<u>Ga</u>	Ma'	Pa	<u>Dha</u>	Ni
10.	Marva	Sa	<u>Re</u>	Ga	Ma	Pa	Dha	Ni

RAGAS

A *Raga* is a combination of sounds or *swaras* having qualities that give pleasure to the listener. Every *Raga* has a peculiar quality of its own. To be acquainted with *Ragas*, a musician should bear in mind the following points :

1. *Ragas* must belong to a *Thaat*.

2. At least five notes are essential for a *Raga*.

3. In a *Raga* the melody is very essential.

4. A *Raga* must have its own ascent, descent (*Aroha* and *avaroha*) and fixed notes *(Vadi & Samvadi)*.

5. The **Sa** *Swara* (C note) is the same note (fixed) in every *Raga*, and both **Ma** & **Pa** are not to be omitted at the same time.

Parts of combination of a Raga

There are 4 distinguished parts of a raga/composition/song.

1. Sthayi	:	First part (face) or introduction.
2. Antara	:	Second part or body.
3. Sanchari	:	Combinarion of notes of *'Sthayi'* & *'Antara'*.
4. Abhog	:	Some notes of the composition played in the upper octave.

Categories of Ragas ('Jati' of a Raga)

The following are the three most common categories of Ragas :

1. **Sampurna** has seven notes ascending and descending.
2. **Shadava** has six notes ascending and descending.
3. **Odava** has five notes in the same *Swaras*, both ascending & descending.

Categories of Ragas

S. No.	Category	No. of Swaras		Total No. of Ragas with the Combination of Ascending & Descending Notes
		Ascent	Descent	
1.	Sampurna–Sampurna	7	7	1 – 1 x 1 – 1
2.	Shadava–Shadava	6	6	6 – 6 x 6 – 36
3.	Odava–Odava	5	5	15 – 15x15– 225
4.	Sampurna–Shadava	7	6	6 – 1 x 6 – 6
5.	Sampurna–Odava	7	5	15 – 1 x 15 – 15
6.	Shadva–Sampurna	6	7	6 – 6 x 1 – 6
7.	Shadva–Odava	6	5	90 – 6 x 15 – 90
8.	Odava–Sampurna	5	7	15 – 15 x 1 – 15
9.	Odava–Shadava	5	6	90 – 15 x 6 – 90

Lay (Tempo or Speed)

LAY : (Tempo)

In the ordinary sense *lay* means Beat or speed or any regular space of time between boundaries to complete a circle in a specific time period. It is a natural harmonious flow of vocal and instrumental sound with a regular succession of accents. There is no fixed structure of speed or tempo in music. Every musician chooses it according to his convenience; but basically, what is important is that one should be able to control the *lay* or tempo of *taal*. The tempo should neither be too slow nor should it be extraordinarily fast. Not only this, even in a slow tempo it should be in such a manner that it can entertain the audience on the one hand and on the other its musicality will not be sacrificed.

Normally a slow tempo should be half the tempo of a standard one and a fast tempo should be double that of the standard. But again it differs according to the capabilitiy of the musician. An expert musician starts the tempo in a very slow pace and gradually increases it reaching the required speed.

According to observations there are mainly three types of beat which have been accepted in the Indian music. But there is one more special type called '*Ati Drut Lay*', which is generally used by expert musicians, because tempo in this particular type is very fast and very tough to control. All percussion instruments are used to control and regularize the musical sound.

The Three types of beats are :

1. **Madhya Lay** (Medium or Normal Beat).
   eg. 1 2 3 4

2. **Drut Lay** (Quick or Fast Beat).
   eg. 1 2 3 4

3. **Vilambit Lay** (Slow Beat).
   eg. 1   2   3   4

(Note the space between the numbers)

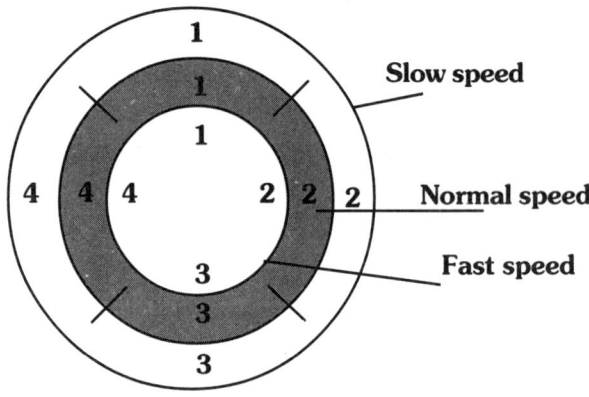

Normal Tempo

Normal Beat is the time required by a musician to complete a round or a part of a song, tune or dance in a comfortable speed without any stress. Although no fix structure is available for this, convenience is the key. The tempo should be easy enough within the musician's control. In a normal speed any composition whether instrumental or vocal leaves a very refreshing effect on the audience. The Normal beat is the basis of the remaining two beats.

Eg. 1 2 3 4 1 2 3 4   etc.

Fast Tempo

Fast Beat means half the time of a normal beat. This is when a musician, say, requires one minute of time to complete a part of a song, tune or dance, in normal beat, now he will require half the time taken by the normal beat. In other words we can say that the musician can take two rounds of his play for the time required in the normal beat.

Eg. 1 2 3 4-1 2 3 4-1 2 3 4 etc.

Slow Tempo

In Slow Beat a musician takes double the time to complete the round required by the medium or normal beat. Suppose if he completes a round of his song in one minute in normal beat, he will now take two minutes to complete the same song.

Eg. 1 - 2 - 3 - 4 - 1 - 2 - 3 - 4   etc.

Comparative speeds in various beats:

Slow beat	: 1			2			3			4		
Medium Beat	: 1	2	3	4		1	2	3	4				
Fast Beat	: 1 2 3 4			1 2 3 4			1 2 3 4			1 2 3 4		

Taal (The Rhythm)

Taal or Rhythm is the regular succession of sound vibrations, necessary to make sound musical. It is a scale for producing the rhythmic pattern in a song or *Raga*. Each song or composition runs on a particular time scale, and the scale is repeated in a particular gap, this gap is repeated for a specific number of times, which makes the rhythm cycle for the composition. The gaps between the notes in a scale is known as intervals, which can be created by clapping, or by a percussion instrument. The most popular is the Tabla. The early Indian musicians invented many *taals* of different *matras* (Rhythms), *Khand* (Bars) and *Bols* (Sounds) and fixed the points of *'Sam', Talis* and *Khalis* for every *Taal*.

Beat : As we know well now, beat is a time-scale map in a composition. The common beats in the Indian system are *Kehrava Taal* (8 beats) and *Daadara taal* (6 beats).

Beat and its part in a composition is written and understood by some technical names like *sam, tali, khali,* etc. in the Indian music system. These terms and names carry a lot of importance for the beginners to understand. Let's learn them in detail.

Bol (Sounds) : Each beat is made out of notes or sounds. These sounds can be of percussions or of melody notes. The sounds created by percussions like drums or tabla, played as accompaniment or are spoken as **Dha, Dhin,** etc. are known as Bols.

Sam : The starting point of a taal notation or a beat cycle, from the point where the beat starts in a composition is known as **Sam.** This is the point in a notation where all the instruments stops and start together when playing many instruments together. It is shown in the notation with **(x)** sign.

Taali : Literally means the clap, it is the particular point in a notation where maximum pressure is given to the playing. This is also the repeated starting point of a part in a beat cycle.

For example; as shown below, while playing "*Teen Taal*" 1ˢᵗ, 5ᵗʰ, & 13ᵗʰ bol has *taali* in its place -

Beat signs	×				2			
Beat	1	2	3	4	5	6	7	8
Bol	Dha	Dhin	Dhin	Dha	Dha	Dhin	Dhin	Dha
Beat signs	0				3			
Beat	9	10	11	12	13	14	15	16
Bol	Dha	Tin	Tin	Ta	Ta	Dhin	Dhin	Dha

Khali : Khali literally means empty space, which is actually not, only the force or emphasis of sound is less in this part. *Khali* in a composition means a gap of some *matras* within *boles* of *Theka* played by the right hand on the Tabla only while the left (*Duggi* or *Dhama*) remains silent in *khali matra* time. This is a point in a notation where comparatively less force is given to the *bol*. For example, while playing "*teen taal*", the 9ᵗʰ beat in the cycle is the space for *khali*.

Parts: Putting all the sounds in a group separated by *sam, tali* and *khali* are known as parts or measures. Parts are shown in notation by a vertical line between the group of notes or sounds. For example: *Daadra taal* is of two parts with 3 sounds per measure:

Beat signs	×			0		
Beat	1	2	3	4	5	6
Bol	Dha	Dhin	Na	Ta	Tin	Na

All the symbols such as *sam, tali, khali* are placed on the 1ˢᵗ note of the group.

Sthayi : First part or the introduction of the song or a composition which is repeated in the song after paragraphs is called *sthayi*.

Antara : The second part or the middle part of the song which is also known as the body is called *Antara*.

Some Important Beats

Keherva Taal

It is the most popular and common *Taal* used in Indian Light Music. It has 8 '*matras*' or beat with **sam** on the 1st beat and **khali** on the 5th. *Ghazal* and *Bhajan* & Light music get beautiful expression in this *taal*. This *taal* is relatively easy to learn and understand and therefore very popular among musicians.

Parts/Measures - 2   Beats - 8
one taali & one Khali

Beat signs	x				0			
Beat	1	2	3	4	5	6	7	8
Bol	Dha	Ge	Na	Ti	Na	Ka	Dhi	Na

Dadra Taal

This is another popular *taal* of Indian Light Music. It consists of 6 *matras* with *sam* on the 1st and *khali* on 5th. Any composition of '*Sringar Ras*' will suit this *taal*. Generally *Thumri*, *Bhajans* and *Ghazals* are sung in this *taal*. This *taal* is very easy to grasp and learn, therefore it is very much in use in the field of music.

Parts/Measures - 2   Beats - 6
one taali & one Khali

Beat signs	×			0		
Beat	1	2	3	4	5	6
Bol	Dha	Dhin	Na	Dha	Tin	Na

Roopak Taal

One of the most popular *taals* of Indian Music; used both in light as well as classical music. It has 7 beats with *sam* on the 1st and *taali* on 5th & 7th *matras*. Some musicians believe that *khali* is on the 1st. Classical compositions as well as light *bhajans* and *ghazals* are made to flourish in this *taal* very extensively. Being a *taal* of odd numbers it is very impulsive and its least numbers of beat make it easier to grasp and control.

Parts/Measures - 3 *Beats - 7*
Two taali & one Khali

Beat signs	×			2		3	
Beat	1	2	3	4	5	6	7
Bol	Tin	Tin	Na	Dhin	Na	Dhin	Na

(**Note :** Roopak taal starts from sam, so the taali is not given there.)

Deep Chandi Taal

This *taal* is usually used in classical music only. It has 14 beats with *sam* on the 1st. This *taal* is generally used by expert musicians. Although light composition can be sung or played in this *taal* but it is not so easy to handle. Medium tempo compositions are used in this *taal*.

Parts/Measures - 4 *Beats - 14*
Three taali & one Khali

Beat signs	×			2			
Beat	1	2	3	4	5	6	7
Bol	Dha	Dhin	S	Dha	Dha	Tin	S
Beat signs	0			3			
Beat	8	9	10	11	12	13	14
Bol	Ta	Tin	S	Dha	Dha	Dhin	S

Teen Taal

This is the base of all *taals* in Indian Music. It has 16 beats with *sam* on 1st, 2nd taali on 5th, *khali* on 9th and 3rd *taali* on 13th. It is called base of all taals because every other *taal* is in the fraction of *teen taal*. It is easy to learn and most widely used in music both light and classical. Slow and medium and fast compositions are played and sung in this *taal*.

Parts/Measures - 4   Beats - 16
Three taali & one Khali

Beat signs	×				2			
Beat	1	2	3	4	5	6	7	8
Bol	Dha	Dhin	Dhin	Dha	Dha	Dhin	Dhin	Dha
Beat signs	0				3			
Beat	9	10	11	12	13	14	15	16
Bol	Dha	Tin	Tin	Ta	Ta	Dhin	Dhin	Dha

Jhap Taal

This *taal* too is very popular but mostly used in classical music. it has 10 matras with *sam* on 1st and 2nd *taali* on 5th, *khali* on 9th and 3rd *taali* on 10th. Composition in slow and medium tempo is generally used in this *taal*. Although light compositions can be made in this *taal* but generally it is not because its rhythm pattern is somewhat different and not so easy to learn and grasp compared to other *taals*.

Parts/Measures - 4   Beats - 10
Three taali & one Khali

Beat signs	×		2		0			3		
Beat	1	2	3	4	5	6	7	8	9	10
Bol	Dhin	Na	Dhin	Dhin	Na	Tin	Na	Dhin	Dhin	Na

Ek Taal

One of the popular *taals* of Indian music system. This *taal* is used in classical music but may be used in light music also. It has 12 *matras* with *sam* on the 1st beat. Slow and fast tempo compositions are used in this *taal*. This *taal* has three times the beat that of *Dadra taal* and hence its rhythm pattern is similar to the later. This *taal* is easy to learn and grasp and is impulsive in nature.

Parts/Measures - 6   *Beats - 12*
Four taali & Two Khali

Beat signs	×		0		2	
Beat	1	2	3	4	5	6
Bol	Dhin	Dhin	DhaGe	TirKit	Tu	Na
Beat signs	0		3		4	
Beat	7	8	9	10	11	12
Bol	Kat	Ta	DhaGe	TirKit	Dhin	Na

Teevra Taal

It is also a popular and old *taal* of Indian music system. Initially it was played on pakhawaj only but now it is widely played in tabla also. Similar to *Roopak* this *taal* has 7 beats. This *taal* is used in classical music only in medium or slow tempo. Its nature is very intense and therefore is used in serious music such as *Dhrupad* and *khayal* etc.

Parts/Measures - 3   *Beats - 7*
Three taali

Beat signs	×			2		3	
Beat	1	2	3	4	5	6	7
Bol	Dha	Din	Ta	Tit	Kat	GaDe	Gin

Indian Music Notation System

Tips to Read a Composition

1. **Shudha Swaras (Full tone Notes):** No sign is required i.e. Sa. Re, Ga, Ma, Pa, Dha, Ni. Only the first letter is required in the notation i.e. S, R, G, M, P, D, N.

2. **Komal Swaras (Half Tone Notes):** A dash (—) is written under the notes i.e. R̲ G̲ D̲ N̲.

3. **Tivra Swara (Sharp Note):** A small perpendicular line is placed over the note i.e. M̍.

4. **Madhya Saptak Swaras (Medium Octave Notes):** No sign is required for this octave notes i.e. S R G M P D N.

5. **Mandra Saptak Swaras (Lower Octave Notes):** A dot is written under the notes i.e. Ṣ Ṛ G̣ Ṃ P̣ Ḍ Ṇ

6. **Ati Mandra Saptak Swaras (Double lower octave):** Two dots are written under the notes i.e. S̤ P̤

7. **Tar Saptak Swaras (Upper Octave Notes):** A dot is written over the notes Ṡ Ṙ Ġ Ṁ Ṗ Ḋ Ṅ

8. **Matras** are shown in numbers 1 2 3 4 5 6 etc. Normally one note shows one *Matra* time.

9. **Tali:** Numbers written between the bars.

10. **Khali:** A Zero (0) is shown in a bar.

11. **Sam:** A sign of (×) is written on the first matra of every *Taal*.

12. **Khand (Bar):** Vertical lines drawn indicating divisions of *Taals*.

13. **Extending or prolonging** of Notes, a dash (—) is written after the notes. One dash shows one matra time.

1st Khand		2nd Khand	3rd Khand
Sam	Tali	Khali	Tali
×	2	0	3
Matras 1 2 3 4	5 6 7 8	9 10 11 12	13 14 15 16

14. Two, Three or Four notes in a ***matra*** time. These notes are combined together by a bracket under the notes i.e. SR SRG SRGM

15. **Jhala (Vamping):** To express *Jhala* normally "J" sign is used. But traditionally and mostly a space is mentioned (–) as *jhala* with notes.

16. **Meend:** Meend is shown by a semicircular line over the notes i.e. SG SM SP.

17. **Chikari:** Small (c) is written after the note. i.e. Sc, Rc, Gc.

18. **Kan Swara (Grace note):** Small letter is written in superscript by the side of the main note on the right.
    $M^G \; P^M$

19. **Prolonging, Pause or Extending the note length:** Dashes are placed after a note, one dash is fixed for one matra time.

    i.e. S—, R— —, G— —.

Format of Music on Sitar

We have learnt about the theory of music and at the same time are familiar with the fundamentals of the music. In other words we now know how to play natural and flat or sharp notes on Sitar. But there is a great confusion when we start playing. After playing the basic notes our mind wonders - what next? What should be played thereafter when we have played so called basics of music. Every instrument has its own unique features and hence every instrument has some fixed protocol according to which they are played. Our Sitar is no exception to this rule. Here, there are certain ways which are fixed and the sitar is played according to that rule only. When we talk about this rule, we find out how music is produced on the sitar which is soothing and appealing to the audience.

Normally the Sitar is a classical instrument on which generally classical music is played, although light music are also played on it. But when we talk about the sitar without any special reference we mean the classical music only. So, let's understand how music is played on the sitar

We start from *"Aalap"*, which is an introduction to a *"Raga"*. *Aalap* is spread in three octaves. Here the artist shows his imagination and different permutation and combination of notes which are used in the *Raga*. After finishing it we start *"Jod"*. *Jod* is a technique in which actual rhythm is not played but it is very much in rhythm. Different tempos are used to play the *Jod*. First of all we start with slow tempo and gradually we increase the speed and play different *"Taans"* also. At a certain speed the tempo of *Jod* becomes so fast that it takes the form of a *"Jhala"*. Again this is the *Jhala* on which no rhythm is played but the *Jhala* itself is a rhythm. This type of *Jhala* is called "*Ulta Jhala*" because it has a slight different pattern compared to the normal *Jhala*. After finishing *Jhala*, the tabla joins in and we play "*Vilambit Gat*". Here the artist shows his mastery over the *Raga* and produces the notes in different melodious combination. Thereafter "*Drut Gat*" is played. In *Drut Gat* the artist shows his command over the speed and tempo. Gradually increasing the speed, the artist finishes with *Jhala*.

Western Notation System

The Western notation system is based on time symbols and where they are placed on the staff. These signs show both the *Swaras* and the length of time. These symbols are the notes, written on a set of 5 horizontal lines and 4 equal spaces between them called the Staff. There are two sets of the staff on which music notes are written: one for the lower tones or sounds and the other for the higher tones or sounds. The **lower tones or pitches** are represented by the **Bass** (*pronounced base*) **Staff** on which the Bass Clef Sign (𝄢) is written and the **higher tones or pitches** and **medium tones or pitches** are represented by the **Treble Staff** on which the Treble clef sign (𝄞) is written. Together these two staves make the **Grand Staff.**

The symbols of notes used in western music and their near meanings in Indian Music are given below.

Symbols of Notes		Sound Values
Whole Note or Semi-breve	o	4 beats (*Matra*) of sound
Half Note or Minim	𝅗𝅥	2 beats (*Matra*) of sound
Quarter Note or Crotchet	♩	1 beat (*Matra*) of sound
Dotted Half Note or Dotted Minim	𝅗𝅥.	3 beats (*Matra*) of sound
Eighth Note or Quaver	♪	½ beat (*Matra*) of sound
16th Note or Semi-quaver	♪	¼ (*Matra*) beat of sound

Symbols of Notes		Sound Values
Full Tone Notes or Naturals	♮	Shudh Swaras (denoted as SRGMPDN)
Half Tone Notes or Flats	♭	Komal Swaras (denotes with line under the note: S RG MP DM)
Sharp Note	♯	Tivra Swara (denote with a vertcal line over the note; SRGṀPDN
Bass Cleff sign	𝄢	Mandra Saptaka (denote with a '•' under the note; S R G M P D N
Treble Cleff sign	𝄞	Tar saptak (denote with a '•' over the notes: S R G M P D N

Apart from the above symbols in western music the beat is also very important. In fact it is the backbone of all music. Without the beat there is no music. The beat in music is related to Time which is Space between measuring units which are numbers. Without numbers we cannot measure time or any form of measurement for that matter. Hence Time maybe defined as space between numbers. So also the beat in music which is **Equal spaces of time between numbers**. These spaces must be equal in music otherwise it is just noise. This means if we have a piece of music that has four beats

the 1st beat will be the **space** between numbers 1 and 2

the 2nd beat will be the **space** between numbers 2 and 3

the 3rd beat will be the **space** between numbers 3 and 4, and

the 4th beat will be the **space** between numbers 4 and 1.

Unlike Indian music western music does not have a **0 beat**, which is called **Khali**. Western music starts on the 1st beat.

The symbols which represent the sounds are called notes. They have sound values to them. When written on the staff, the note symbols represent the different lengths of sound, thus, making the rhythm of music. Rhythm may then be defined as the combination of all the long and short sounds in a piece of music within a specific beat. In other words the combination of all the different kinds of notes in a piece of music. There are basically four types of Rhythm from which all music is written. These are as follows:

1. A rhythm where the sound is more than one beat (single space of time) or in other words a note represents two or more beats of sound.

2. A rhythm where the sound is equal to one beat (single space of time) or a note represents one beat of sound.

3. A rhythm where the single beat (single space of time) will have two sounds which means that the beat is divided into two sounds which are equal in length.

4. A rhythm where the single beat (space of time) will have three or four or more sounds within the beat and these are also equally divided.

Western music is also divided into sections or divisions which we call Measures which are formed by vertical lines on the staff which we call Bar Lines. The beat in western music is grouped normally in double, triple, or quadruple time that is 2, 3 or 4 beats per measure. We find this in the time signature which is a set of two numbers one above the other. These numbers are normally found in the beginning of a piece of music.

Just as we speak in sentences to make sense in music we also have musical sentences which we call phrases and which normally consist of four measures of sound but which may also vary depending on the composition. These musical sentences are marked by curved lines called Slurs. These lines are found over a set of notes on the staff which indicate the phrase of music which expresses an idea. A complete sentence would normally consists of two phrases, the first called the **statement** and the second the **response**. These musical phrases or sentences usually end in a form of punctuation which we call **cadences** in music. They denote the end of a phrase.

All music is based on scales hence scales are the skeleton or backbone of any musical composition. In western music we have two basic kinds of scales - the Major scales and the Minor scales. The Minor scales are of three types - these are Natural minor, the Harmonic minor and the Melodic minor scales. Scales are built on a pattern of Tones and semitones. These tones and semitones are the distances of sounds. The semitones are the closest distance of two notes or pitches while the tones are two semitones side by side. Basing on the pattern of tones and semitones scales are identified as whether they are sharp scales or flat scales. A **sharp scale** is when the natural note of the scale is *raised* by a semitone and a **flat scale** is when the natural note of the scale is *lowered* by a semitone.

For example:
G major the notes are   G A B C D E F$^\#$ G
F major the notes are   F G A B$^\flat$ C D E F

All together we have about sixty scales in western music, these include all the majors and their relative minors, in all 3 forms. The ***number of sharps or flats*** in them we call the **key signature** of a scale. This includes the three types of minor scales as mentioned earlier. One may compare scales to multiplication tables in school which need to be learnt if we want to understand music properly. They are most essential in music learning.

Another very important aspect of western music is the skill of reading music which is most important if one is to be a good musician. For this we learn to identify **notes** on the staff, that is the lines and spaces, by the **distances** between them as they are **written on the staff,** up or down the staff. We call this Intervals between notes. We know that there are eight notes to a scale hence we number them as 1 2 3 4 5 6 7 8 or call them the eight degrees of a scale. Basing on this we identify the intervals between notes written on the lines and spaces. The following are the intervals identified.

1. Repeat - This is the interval of notes on the same line or space on the staff.
   eg. Notes on the same second line or same third space.
2. Second - (Step) - The interval from a line note to a space note up or down.
   eg. Notes on the 1st line and the 1st space up or notes on the 4th space and 4th line down.
3. Third - (Skip) - The interval from a line note to the next line note or from a space note to the next space note up or down.
   eg. 3rd line note to 4th line note up or 2nd space note to 1st space note down.
4. Fourth - (3rd + 2nd) - The interval from a line note to a space note or space note to a line note up or down with a space and line in between.
   eg. 1st line note to 2nd space note up or 4th line note to 2nd space note down.
5. Fifth - (3rd + 3rd) - The interval from a line note to a line note or space note to a space note up or down with a line or space in between.
   eg. 1st line note to 3rd line note up or 3rd space note to 1st space note down.

Interval reading helps in getting the right pitch (sound) and the correct finger to play on the instrument. This skill of reading is most helpful for a smooth flowing production of sound on any instrument.

Points To Remember for Combined Notation System

Before using combined notation system the musicians should bear the following points in mind.

1. **The middle point C is fixed for every song, *Raga* or tune. The Sa or C note is compulsory. All tunes are based on the C note.**
2. **G note [P] cannot be changed into a half tone (flat) or a sharp note.**
3. **P and F cannot be omitted at a time in any *Raga*.**

The Symbol of matra on the staff notation is accepted by our combined notation system. It is equal to one *matra* time. Symbols of No. 1 and No. 2 are not used in combined notation system. The remaining fractional *matra* time symbols may be used as they are. The position of symbol of time notes in the clefs are accepted as they are.

Symbols of half tone notes (flats) and the sharp note are accepted. The symbol of extension of sound [—] is accepted for prolonging the notes, not for ending the sound. This symbol denotes one matra time. The symbol of prolonging notes for meend without dots are accepted as [ ] and for combined notes as [ ].

In the Indian Music system there are a number of taal variations which are not used in western music. Not only this, western music uses the taal with evenly spaced numbers only but in Indian music we have a number of taals which are odd and very complicated to play and understand. The notation of these taals and compositions set to these taals are naturally very hard to grasped.

There are a number of expressions such as 1.75 times of a beat, or .25 times of a beat, or 2.75 of a beat in Indian music notation system.

These expressions should be understood in Indian system only and be mastered in order to have a better command over the music of any form.

Part - 2
The Sitar - Then & Now

History and Development

The sitar is recognized as a popular Indian musical instrument. Its speciality is that its resonator is a gourd and its sympathetic strings sound without playing them. It is a long fingerboard string instrument and is played primarily on one string.

The Sitar, an instrument from classical times, is believed to have its origin from ancient Greece as the **Kithara** or the Roman Empire or may be both. It is believed to have gotten its design from the Persian lute, which would tell us how it derived its name, **Sehtar**, an Arabic origin meaning seven strings. Today it is a *Hindustani* musical instrument made from a special

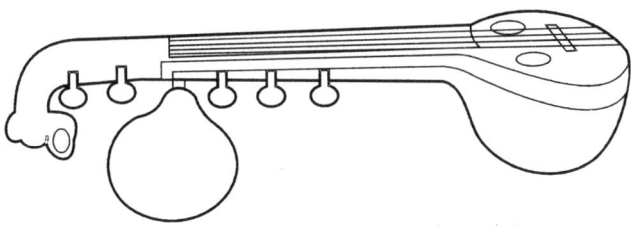

gourd. The Sitar is an improved version of the *Veena*, an old and prominent Indian classical musical instrument. Its resonant chamber is the gourd.

It is believed that the invention of the sitar goes to Amir Khusru. Amir Khusru has been given the credit for the early development of *Hindustani Sangeet* (North Indian classical music). He lived during the 13th century AD. As common as this story exists, there is no basis or historical fact. The Sitar was clearly nonexistent until the fall of the *Moghul* Empire.

We know for certain today that the Sitar developed in the Indo-Pakistan subcontinent at the end of the Moghul era. We also know today that it evolved from the Persian lute that was played in the Moghul courts for hundreds of years. The *"Sangeet Sudarshana"* states that the sitar was invented in the 18th century by a *fakir* named Amir Khusru. A different Amir Khusru from the one who lived in the Thirteenth century. This latter Amir Khusru, a 15th

descendent of Naubat Khan, the son-in-law of Tansen, is believed to have developed todays' sitar from the Persian *Sehtar*.

Amir khusru's grandson, Masit Khan, is considered as one of the most influential musicians in the development of the Sitar. He was the one who composed numerous slow gats in the *Dhrupad* style. This style is referred to as the *Masitkhani Gat*. These gats were popularized by his son, Bahadur Khan.

Masit Khan was a resident of Delhi, hence these *Masitkhani Gats* are sometimes called *Dilli Ka Baaj*.

Raza Khan was another influence in the development of sitar music. Raza Khan, a descendent of Tansen, lived in Lucknow around 1800-1850 AD. He was also known as Ghulam Raza. It was he who developed the fast *gat* known as the *Razakani gat*.

Amrit Sen and Rahim Sen have been credited for modifying the tuning and stringing of the Sitar. They also introduced numerous new techniques for playing the instrument.

Though the exact date of its development has not yet been traced, it has been proved beyond doubt that it was first evolved by making improvements on the *Veena* in the 14th century. It is certain now that the present sitar emerged in the Eighteenth century with the addition of three extra strings to the *sehtar*.

At first it contained only 3 strings and was called *Sehtar* (Three-stringed instrument). For a long time the *Sehtar* could not find its proper place in the community of musicians. So the *Veena Vadan* gained popularity. With the passage of time *Sehtar Vadan* became quite popular with the musical audience. It's sweet clink and melodious sound enraptured and enchanted the public and gradually the *Sehtar* found its proper place. Later on the *Sehtar* was given seven strings. With this it became more developed and could produce sweeter and more melodious sounds.

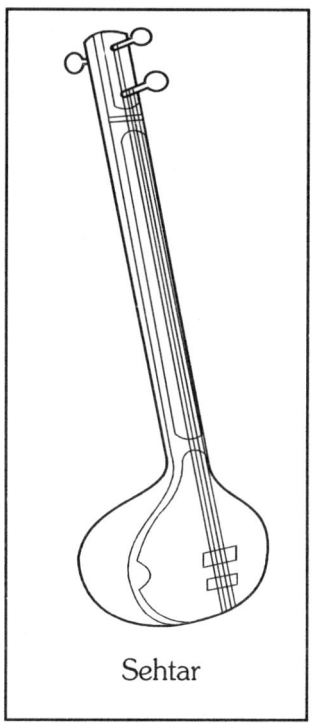

Sehtar

Indian String Instruments

According to ancient Indian scriptures there was only one string instrument known as the 'Veena'. As we know by history that most of the string instruments originated from the Veena, the amalgamation of Iranian and middle eastern instrument to it divided the 'Veena' in two known types. These are **Tat** and **Vitat**, which literally means: **Plucked** and **Unplucked** respectively.

The **Tat** types of string instruments are either plucked or hammered. It includes maximum number of instruments of lute and harp types such as :

1. Sitar
2. Rabab(Kabuli Rabab)
3. Sarod
4. Saraswati Vina
5. Surbahar
6. Gotuvadyam
7. Rudra Vina
8. Vichitra Vina
9. Ektar
10. Tanpura
11. Dotar
12. Santur
13. Surmandal
14. Bulbul Tarang
15. Nakula Vina
16. Magadi Vina
17. Gettuvadyam
18. Gopichand(Ektar)
19. Seni Rabab

The next type is the **Vitat**, which are bowed instruments. These were not traditionally known but a recent addition to Indian music. These are such as follows:

1. Saringda
2. Esraj
3. Dilriba
4. Chikara
5. Mayuri Vina
6. Sarangi
7. Violin

Some String Instruments, and how they look like:

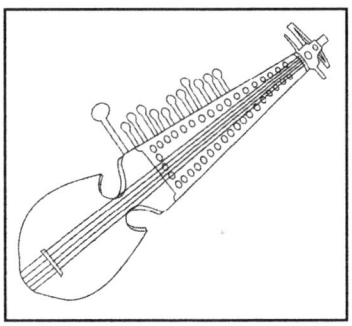

Rabab(Kabuli Rabab)

Kabuli Rabab is a fretless instrument and believed to have come from Kabul, Afghanistan. This instrument is predecessor of Sarod as believed by scholars.

SAROD

Sarod is the most popular fretless instrument of Indian Music. It has a number of strings depending upon the style and make of the instument. It is used in classical musical rendition as well as in light music.

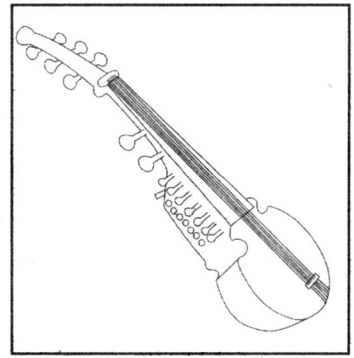

Tanpura

Tanpura is a popular drone instrument of Indian Music, both North Indian and Carnatic. It has four or five strings.

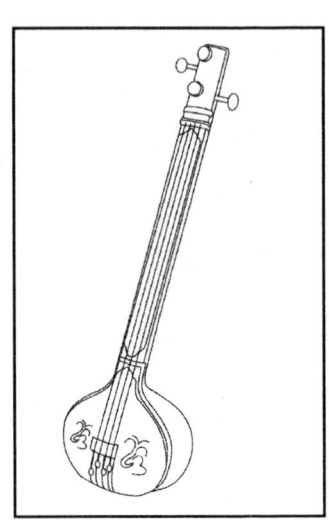

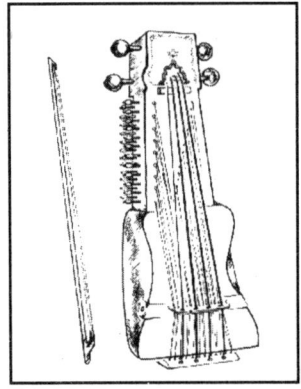

Sarangi

Sarangi is a fretless instrument very close to human voice. It is very popular in classical as well as light music.

Violin

It is also a fretless instrument with four strings. It is used in classical as well as light music.

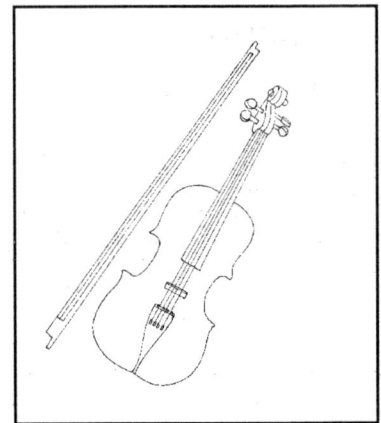

Surmandal

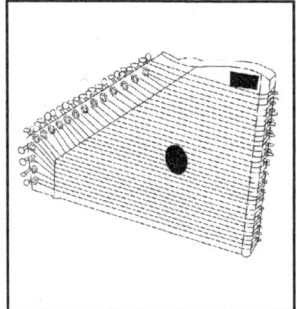

Surmandal is an instrument with so many strings tuned to various notes. It is used in classical musical rendition and acts as a drone instrument.

Santoor

Santoor is a known as hundred stringed instrument. It is used mostly in classical as well as light music.

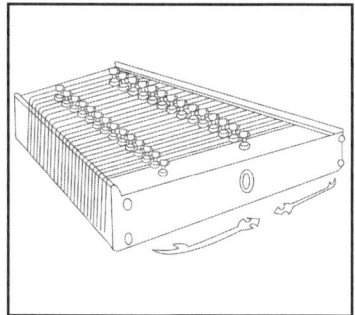

Out of these two types of plucked and bowed instruments, some are not Indian instruments but are influences from westernisation of music. All these instruments have the capacity to play Indian rhythms and ragas. The most popular amongst them are the Sitar and Veena. The Veena vadan is understood to be less popular as it is 'too classical', or perhaps because speed on the Veena has limitations as compared to the sitar or sarod. Not only this, some feel that the Sitar has more sweetness and better sound quality. Sitar playing to this benefit gained popularity in the west because of its ease in playing and rich tonal quality due to the sympathetic strings.

Famous Sitarists

The person responsible for its popularity in the west is **Pt. Ravi Shankar**. He comes from a Bengali Brahmin community in Benaras. In 1938 he started his formal training under Ustad Allauddin Khan. He spent a number of years in learning the sitar under the able tutelage of Ustad Allaudin khan, popularly known as 'Baba' and later pursued his own professional career. His unique playing style with exemplary command over the rhythm. He came as a thunderbolt in the field of music and left the audience spellbound with his amazing performances. He has won many awards including the Bharat Ratna, several Grammy awards and numerous honorary Doctorates.

Another well known name in re-establishing the sitar in India is **Ustad Vilayat Khan**. He is known for playing the "Gayaki Ang" on the sitar. Born into a musical family in 1924, he had become one of the most influential musicians of the 20th century. His maternal uncle Zinda Hussain Khan taught him the sitar in 1930. He had an extensive professional career. He refused the *Padmabhushan,* one of India's top civilian honors. The only title that he embraced was the title *Aftab-e-Sitar* (Sun of the Sitar). He died of lung cancer on March 13th, 2004. He was 76 years of age.

Other Sitarists of these modern times are:

1. **Pandit Nikhil Banerjee** was one of India's most prominent Sitar masters of the 20th Century. Nikhil Banerjee was born in Calcutta 14 October 1931 into a Brahmin family. His father, Jitendranath Banerjee, who was a Sitarist as his hobby, taught him on the instrument.

   In 1947 Banerjee met Allauddin Khan, who was to become his main guru along with his son Ali Akbar Khan. Allauddin Khan passed on to his students not only playing technique but the musical knowledge and approach of the Maihar gharana. Under his teaching, Shankar and Banerjee developed different sitar styles.

   His interpretation of ragas was always highly traditional. He created a raga Manomanjari of his own, mixing ideas from Kalavati and Marwa.

   In 1968, he was decorated with the Padma Shri and posthumously received also the Padma Bhushan. He died on 27 January 1986 of a heart attack.

2. **Pt. Debu Chaudhary:** He is also a senior artist of India. He has the credit of playing the sitar of 17 frets with his own style of playing. He is still doing a lot to promote the Sitar and Indian music in the country and abroad. His reputation as a guru and performing artist is a milestone for upcoming music lovers and a lot can be learnt from his prosperous wealth of music.

3. **Pt. Buddhatiya Mukherjee:** Disciple of Ustaad Vilayat Khan, Pt. Buddhatiya Mukherjee has a uniform place in the field of sitar. A well known player of the modern times, he is credited with many awards.

4. **Ustaad Shujat Khan:** Shujaat Husain Khan is a distinguished Indian musician and sitar player. He belongs to the Imdad Khan gharana of the sitar.

   Shujaat Husain Khan is the son and disciple of master sitarist Ustad Vilayat Khan. From a tender age he has performed in all prestigious music festivals in India and has traveled around the world. Shujaat Husain Khan has developed his own unique style of playing Indian classical music. He is also known for his exceptional voice, which he uses for singing folk songs and poetry.

   He has been invited as visiting faculty at the Dartington School of Music in England, the University of Washington in Seattle and the University of California at Los Angeles.

   He has over 50 musical releases on a variety of international labels. Additionally, he has been honored with numerous awards by many different Indian and international organizations.

5. **Ustaad Shahid Parvez:** Ustad Shahid Parvez Khan belongs to the Etawah gharana in sitar playing. Ustad Shahid Parvez was introduced to vocal music and tabla by his illustrious father, Ustad Aziz Khan, before he was initiated into playing sitar.

   In Ustad Shahid Parvez, we find a unique combination of the 'gayaki' ang and the 'tantrakari' ang. Ustad Shahid Parvez is a 'top' grade artist of All India Radio. He is one of the few maestros to enjoy global reputation, and he has numerous LP records, audio and video cassettes, and Compact Discs to his credit. He has been honored with several awards, both national and international, and has participated in many of the major festivals in India and abroad, including the Festival of India, held in the U.S., Canada, U.S.S.R., Europe, and so on.

6. **Ustad Rais Khan :** Ustad Rais Khan was born in Indore, Madhya Pradesh, India in 1939. His family background descends through 30 generations of Indian culture. Ustad Rais Khan descends directly from court musicians of 15th Century Moghul Emperors, thus he belongs to one of the oldest and most renowned musical families and is therefore the torchbearer of a lineage that dates back to Haddu Khan and Hassu Khan. His father, Ustad Mohammed Khan started his son's "Taalim" (training) at the age of two and a half. At the age of five he gave his first public performance. From there he never looked back.

His dynamic personality and genius have made him one of the most outstanding artists of our time. The fact that he is an accomplished vocalist accounts for much of his popularity. At the end of his recitals he often sings and demonstrates compositions which thrills his listeners. Through these demonstrations his audiences are able to see immediately how closely related vocal and instrumental music are.

His music is his life and his links with his audiences are his life-blood. He has a number of records and LPs to his credit and a long list of awards.

7. **Shri Kushal Das :** Kushal Das, a north Indian solo sitarist was born to a highly enriched musical family of Calcutta.

Kushal started his talim from the age of seven. He received intensive and rigorous training in advanced sitar techniques and the art of music making under the affectionate guidance of Prof. Sanjoy Bandopadhyay, the renowned sitar maestro and academician. He also had the proud privilege of having learnt from great musicians like, Pt. Manas Chakraborty, Pt. Ramkrishna Basu and Late Pt. Ajoy Sinha Roy.

Kushal Das is a musician with vast experience of performing in so many musical concerts all over India and every corner of the world. He is also the recipient of so many awards.

8. **Ustaad Halim Zafar Khan:** One of the extra ordinary maestros of the Sitar of the 21st Century is Ustaad Halim Zafar Khan who became synonymous with the Sitar. He has gained great name and fame for himself.

9. **Pt. Mor Mukut kedia:** A young and dynamic sitar maestro of modern time. Disciple of Ustaad Ali Akbar Khan, Guru Maa Annapurna Devi and Pt. Sunil Mukherjee. He has a very sweet style of playing with remarkable mastery over the intricacies of lay, sur and taal. He is the recipient of many awards and has the honor of performing in all the major music festivals of the Country with great maestros like Pt. Kishan Maharaj and Ustaad Zakir Hussain. He is capable of giving new dimensions to the sitar.

❋ ❋ ❋ ❋

Part - 3
Know The Sitar

Various Types of Sitar

The Sitar of today has seven strings on the upper part for playing and eleven or sometimes thirteen sympathetic strings under the frets.

With these additions we can broadly say that there are Three types of Sitars these are:

1. Single Sitar

2. Standard Sitar with sympathetic strings.

3. Standard double gourd sitar with sympathetic strings

Lets understand the three types of the Sitar.

Single Sitar has seven strings on top without sympathetic strings. This type of Sitar is useful for beginners. As this sitar does not have sympathetic strings it is much easier to tune and therefore easy to play. But this type of sitar lacks the natural vibration of sound which is the distinct quality of a sitar.

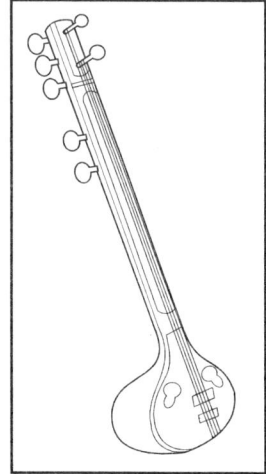

Single Sitar

The **Standard Sitar** has seven strings on the upper part and eleven or thirteen sympathetic strings under the frets. This is generally used by Sitarists of a particular school. Qualitatively there is no difference in this type and the double gourd type sitar. It only differs in its looks. Some claim that the double gourd has more resonance than this sitar.

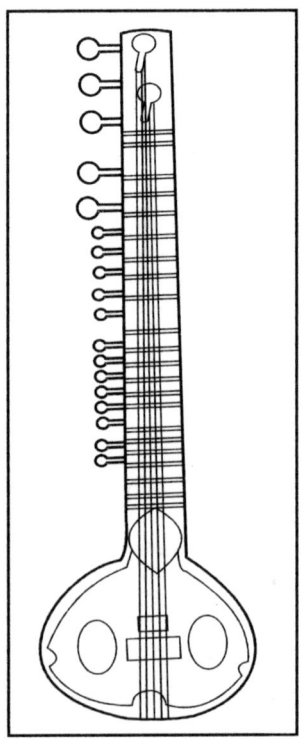

Standard Sitar
(With Sympathetic Strings) →

The **Double Gourd Sitar** has seven strings including chikaris on the upper portion and eleven or thirteen sympathetic strings under the frets, just like the Standard Sitar. The difference between the two is the additional gourd fixed on its top behind the upper bridge. This gourd is smaller than the main gourd and helps in giving extra resonance to the lower octave notes. It also adds beauty and makes the instrument look more like the 'Veena'.

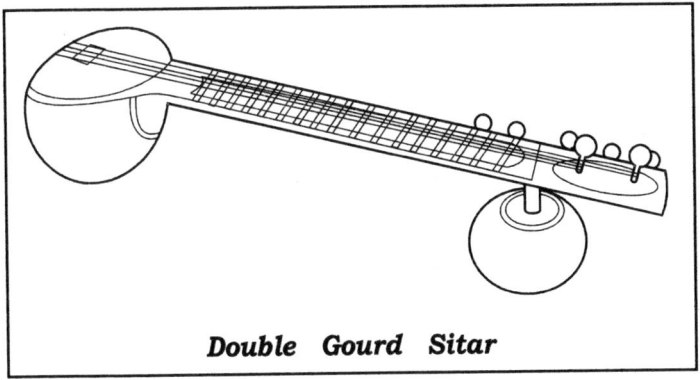

Double Gourd Sitar

These days the Sitar has become more popular especially among women sitarists. In western countries too the Sitar has taken an appreciable place in the circle of musicians.

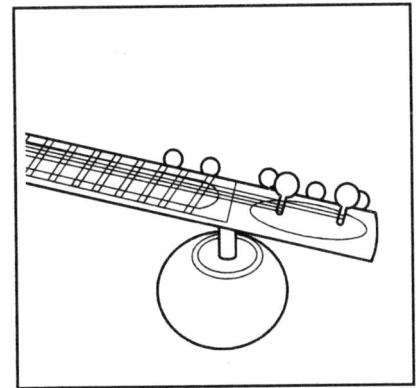

Parts of a Sitar

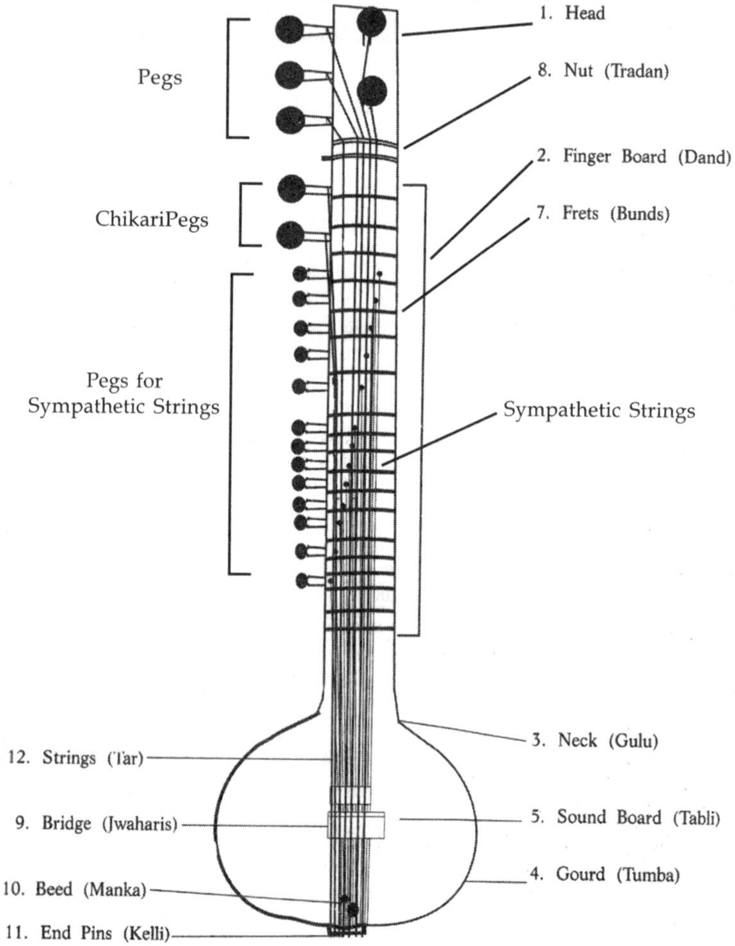

- 1. Head
- 8. Nut (Tradan)
- 2. Finger Board (Dand)
- 7. Frets (Bunds)
- Pegs
- ChikariPegs
- Pegs for Sympathetic Strings
- Sympathetic Strings
- 3. Neck (Gulu)
- 12. Strings (Tar)
- 9. Bridge (Jwaharis)
- 5. Sound Board (Tabli)
- 4. Gourd (Tumba)
- 10. Beed (Manka)
- 11. End Pins (Kelli)

Parts of a Sitar

1. **Head *(Sheesh)***: The top portion of the finger board is called the head. On the Head the five main strings are attached to pegs firmly. This is a single wooden piece attached to the lower wooden piece of the finger board.

2. **Sound Board *(Tabli)***: It is a kind of wooden plate of Tun-wood fixed to the top of the *Tumba* (Gourd). It is the main part of the Sitar that produces the sound. The thickness of the soundboard effects the quality of the sound.

3. **Neck (Gulu)**: It is a small piece of Tun Wood in the shape of a neck. It joins the Gourd *Tumba* and the finger board *(Dand)*. Gullu plays an important role in sitar making as it is one part which is most used by the player for keeping the thumb on while playing.

4. **Gourd *(Tumba)***: It is a big dry pumpkin which is hollow inside. The one prominent feature of a sitar. It is made after selecting one from many chosen pumpkins. This is used as a resonating chamber of the Sitar.

5. **Finger Board (Dand)**: These are two pieces of Tun wood, one upper and the other lower. The upper part is a flat piece of wood joined with another hollow piece of wood. The upper part contains thirteen holes for Tarabs or Sympathetic strings and their pegs. It is well polished and varnished to have a clean, dust-free surface, which helps the resonance of the sound on the soundboard.

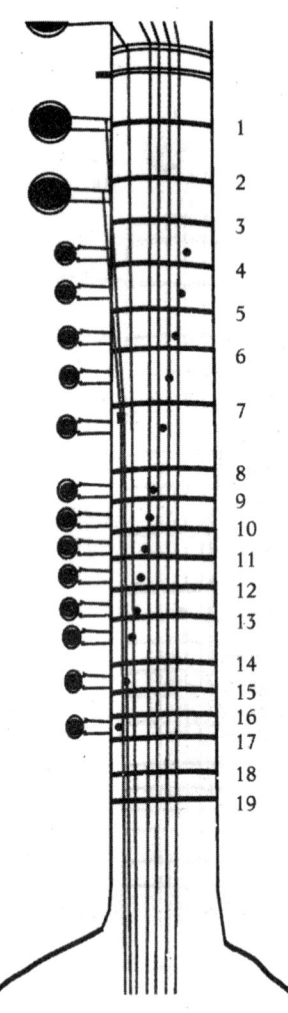

The Finger board of the Sitar is also known as the *Dand*. It is the portion of the instrument where all the notes are played.

Also on the finger board are holes for sympathetic strings with pegs. There are normally 11 holes but sometimes there are 13 also.

The upper end of the finger board is called the bridge from where the strings pass. The lower end is known as the neck or Gullu, which separates the playing portion of the Sitar from the sound portion, the Gourd.

6. **Pegs (*Gatte*)**: The pegs are used for tuning the strings of the sitar. They are normally made of *Shisham* or Teak wood. Two sizes of pegs are commonly used. One is big, for the main strings and the others are small, for the sympathetic strings. Small holes are bored in the pegs to attach the strings. These pegs are fixed in the holes of the *Dand*.

7. **Frets(*Bunds*)**: These are nickel plated brass-rods tied to the finger board with nylon threads. Their sequence is from the upper to the lower part of the Sitar. The number of frets varies from 18 to 20 frets. These are the stops for creating notes on the sitar.

8. **Nylon threads *(Tandi)*** : They are made of nylon. These threads that tie the frets on to the fingerboard. They are neither tight nor loose so they can be adjusted by pulling up and down.

9. **Nut *(Tardan)***: It is an ivory piece fixed on the upper part of the *Dand*. Cuttings are made according to the number and size of the strings. Strings are first passed over the nut and through the hole of the adjuster container and tied to the pegs. Keeping the nuts clean for a hassle free passage of the strings through it is mandatory.

10. **Bridge *(Jawaharis)*:** Two sizes of Bridges are used in a Sitar, one is big, used for the upper strings and the other is small for the *Tarabs* (sympathetic strings). They are made of ivory. The overtones of the sitar are produced by the vibration of the strings against the bridge.

11. **Beads *(Manka)*:** These are made of ivory or bone and used specially for fine tuning of a sitar. It is done to tighten the string by moving it forward or back. The first string of the sitar is called *Baj* or *Madhyam*. It passes through both the Bridges placed on top of the sound board. The top or the bigger bead is made of bone or ivory and it is placed on top of a wooden Bridge. The small Bridge is for the first bead usually swan shape. The Bead is placed between the bridge and the end-pin. The second string passes through a normal oval shape bead.

12. **Chikari bridge *(Mogra or Killiyan)*** : These are small sticks made of ivory or plastic and stand perpendicular over the fingerboard near the chikari pegs. The purpose of these raisers is to pull up the chikari strings to the level of the strings that are fixed to this bridge which passes over it.

13. **End Pins (Kelli)**: These are ivory pins fixed to the Toe of the Sitar. It is on the end-pins that all the strings of the sitar are tied. It holds the pressure pull of the strings. Its firmness is very important because if it is not strong enough, it may break the tumba of the sitar and damage it.

14. **Strings (Tar):** There are 7 strings on the Sitar on the upper part which are for playing. Out of these seven, 4 are made of steel and 3 of bronze. Besides these strings 11 or 13 sympathetic steel strings are also attached on the portion below the main strings of the finger board, under the frets. Of these seven strings the first one is the most important. This is the string on which all the important notes are played when plucking it with the help of mizrab.

15. **Mizrab:** It is the plectrum for the sitar made from a single piece of rather thick iron wire, which is used to pluck the strings of the sitar. It is shaped into a triangle that should fit snugly and firmly on to the tip of the right index finger. The long, pointed metal wire is worn over the nail of the index finger passing over the tip and under the pad of the finger. The wire's 'V' at the sides need to be placed over the index finger's sides. A correct size mizrab will hold firmly on to the first joint of the index finger.

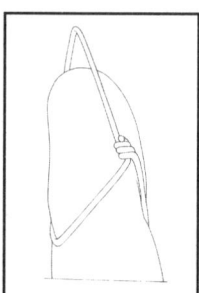

Strings & Frets

There are normally two sets of strings in a Sitar. The main strings are 7, which are for playing; 4 of steel and 3 of bronze. Each main string has a name and they are originally tuned to a particular note, that is if played without keeping the finger on the frets. These open strings give the sound of these notes:

String No.	Name	Note
String 1	*Baj tar*	Ma
String 2 & 3	*Jora*	S
String 4	*Laraj*	P
String 5	*Kharaj*	S
String 6	*Chikari* 1	S
String 7	*Chikari* 2	Sa

Sympathetic strings: The strings behind the main strings are called sympathetic strings, which are 11 to 13 in number and are not to be played with strokes of the *Mizrab*. They are thin steel strings. These strings produce sounds because of the vibrations produced by the main strings. They are also called resonant strings. They are tuned according to the notes used in the raga, so that when the main string is played the corresponding sympathetic string will vibrate sympathetically like a support to echo the sound of that particular note. Sympathetic strings are used in musical instruments to enhance their sound. They are sometimes played by using the raised nail of the fourth finger.

Frets: There are normally 19 frets tied to the fingerboard. Some players use an extra fret. The frets are used as stop points for playing various notes.

Strings Sizes and Types:

Main string: The following is a self explanatory ready reference chart for the seven main string.

Sympathetic strings : All Sympathetic strings in the Sitar are steel strings with gauge 33 or 34

String No.	Metal	Gauge
1.	Steel	30
2.	Bronze	27 or 28
3.	Bronze	27 or 28
4.	Steel	30 or 32
5.	Bronze	21 or 26
6.	Steel	33 or 34 (Chikari No.1)
7.	Steel	33 or 34 (Chikari No.2)

❋ ❋ ❋ ❋

Part – 4
Playing The Sitar

Sitting Positions

Position 1: Traditional Indian Style

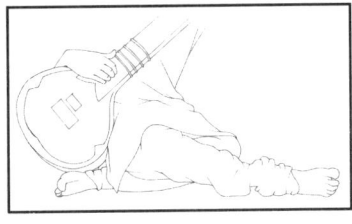

In this posture of playing the Sitar both the knees are bent inside. The *Tumba* (Gourd) is supported by the right thigh. It is held by the elbow of the right hand and the Sitar is positioned diagonally in front of the player. The *Mizrab* is played by the first finger of the right hand and the thumb rests on the finger board *(Dand)*. The fingers of the left hand move over the Frets *(band)*. This posture is common with women Sitarists.

When comfortably sitting in this position, keep the sitar on your right side supporting the Gourd *(Tumba)* against the right hip, over the left foot. The left foot and right thigh should support the sitar diagonally upwards. It should be held by the elbow and thumb of the right hand.

Position 2: Both Knees Bent Inside

In this posture of playing Sitar both the knees are bent. The *Tumba* (Gourd) is supported by the right thigh. It is held by the elbow of the right hand and the Sitar is positioned diagonally in front of the player. The *Mizrab* is played by the first finger of the right hand and the thumb rests on the finger board *(Dand)*. The fingers of the left hand move over the Frets *(band)*. This posture is common among women.

Position 3: Playing on a Chair or Bench

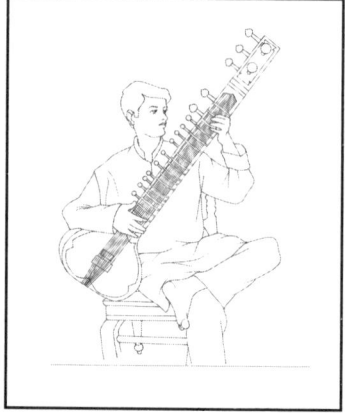

In the third posture the player sits on a bench or on an armless chair of comfortable height. The right leg is placed over the left leg and the *Tumba* is supported beside the right thigh or on the edge of the chair. It is held in position by the elbow of the right hand and thumb. The Sitar is positioned diagonally upwards.

This position is not a traditional position and not recommended for beginners, players use this position in a concert or at a place where they are unable to sit on the floor.

Important Tips While Playing the Sitar

Now that we have the sitting postures for playing Sitar it is your choice to select any of them according to your liking and convenience. Keep the instrument in the proper way according to your posture choice. Now there are some important tips to follow while playing the sitar.

TIP 1

Hold the Sitar with the right hand pressing the instrument with the arm on the neck and gourd. The thumb will rest on the back of the fret-board.

TIP 2

The Position of the finger board should be at 45^0 or as convenient to the sitting position.

TIP 3

The Sitar should have the support of the right hand. The left hand fingers are to move freely over the fretboard.

TIP 4

The player should play the left hand fingers between the frets and the thumb on the back on the finger board. Position the instrument (finger board) close to the body. Judge the placement of the fingers by looking at the back of the fingerboard.

TIP 5

The left hand thumb moves with the movement of the fingers on the frets.

TIP 6

The left thumb only presses lightly on the back of the finger board, directly parallel to the index finger and moves up and down with the finger.

TIP 7

The left fingers should not press the string directly over the top of the fret. The tip of the fingers should press on the string between the frets.

TIP 8

Normally the **first** and **second fingers** are used. They should hold gently and be relaxed.

❋ ❋ ❋ ❋

Part - 5
Sounds and Notes

Production of Basic Bols

There are two types of sounds produced by the sitar. Bols, which are the basic sounds of the sitar, are produced by the right hand stroke on the string and Notes, which are played by pressing the fingers on the frets, along with the bols.

Bols on Sitar

The first finger of the right hand is used for striking the strings and a *Mizrab* is used for this purpose. The *mizrab* is worn on the first finger of the right hand. It should fit snugly at the fingertip so that it does not move when playing the instrument. The thumb supports the hand over the fretboard and the palm hangs loose over the strings. This makes striking the string easy for the finger.

The *bols* by the *Mizrab* are fixed on the Sitar for *Gats* and *Toras*. These are: Da, Ra and Dir. Other *Bols* are played with the combination of the above three *Bols. i.e.* Dar, Rda, DirDa.

Da Bol

When the Mizrab strikes the first string in the inward direction as closing the palm, it is called Da. The first finger strikes the string while the other fingers support providing force to the stroke. So the 'Da' Bol is striking the Mizrab on the first string in the **inward** direction.

Ra Bol

When the Mizrab strikes on the first string in the outward direction as opening the palm, it is called Ra. The first finger strikes the string while the other fingers support providing force to the stroke. So 'Ra' Bol is striking the Mizrab on the first string in the **outward** direction.

Dir Bol

When the mizrab strikes on the first string rapidly inward and outward, it is called Dir. Dir is a combination of Da and Ra bol played in quick motion. So Dir sound is a rapid playing of the two Bols **Da + Ra = Dir.**

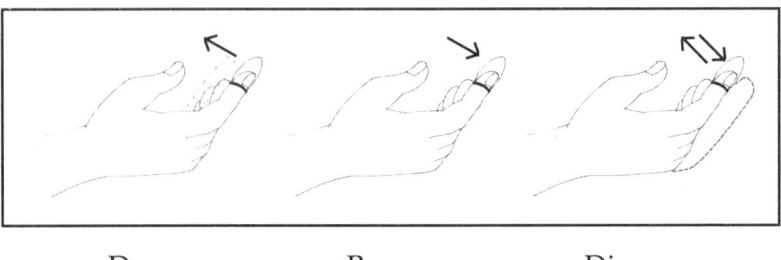

Da   Ra   Dir

Tips for Playing Sounds

TIP 1	When the first finger strikes the other three fingers move together with the first finger, inward and outward.
TIP 2	The *Mizrab* strikes only the string that is to be played.
TIP 3	When playing Da, Ra and Dir the left hand first finger remains on fret no. 7, the Sa note.

Jhala

Jhala is a very important ornamental technique in Sitar playing. It is usually played at the end of a composition or sometimes after the *Alaap*. It is played at a fast tempo and also used to fill gaps between empty spaces within a composition, to make the composition more attractive.

Jhala is played on the Chikari strings along with the main string. The stroke on these strings are always a 'Ra' sound (palm open) together on both strings.

The normal *jhala* sounds are three consecutive strikes on the chikari strings followed by the 'Da' bol of the right hand playing any desired note. Played as:

Da -	Ra Ra Ra	Da -	Ra Ra Ra
(as Sa on 1ˢᵗ string)	(*Jhala* on chikari strings)	(as Sa on 1ˢᵗ string)	(*Jhala* on chikari strings)

Jhala can be played in four different ways. These are *Ekal* (single) *Jhala*, *Yugma* (double) *Jhala*, *Mishrit* (mixed) *Jhala* and *ulta* (reverse) *Jhala*.

Tips for playing *Jhala*

TIP 1	*Jhala* playing is always started by a 'Da' *bol*.
TIP 2	*Jhala* is a technique of fast tempo and sounds good in medium, fast and very fast tempo.
TIP 3	One or both strings can be struck together.
TIP 4	The left hand is used to play the desired note or some times only 'Sa' note on the 'Da' sound while playing *the Jhala*.

Position of Notes on Frets

There are normally 19 frets tied to the fingerboard of the Sitar, but can be increased by one at the bottom to make it 20, for an additional note of the higher octave. Three of the frets are movable to lower the sound and make the natural note a flat note.

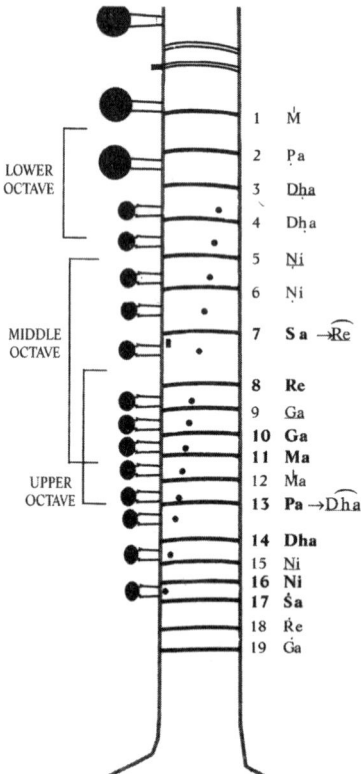

According to the placement of the frets, the fingerboard is divided into three octaves. Starting at the top, the first six frets play the lower octave notes - M,M,P,D,D,N,N. Fret no. 7 to 16 complete the middle octave notes (except komal Re & Dha) and fret 17 to 19, the Higher octave notes S,R,G.

The fingerboard produces most of the notes on the frets. The remaining notes are played either by meend* technique or by moving the frets upward. Notes like Komal Re & Dha of the middle octave are produced using meend from their previous notes or by moving their frets from shuddha swaras.

---

* Meend is a technique of pulling down the string from its origional position to produce the next note of the fret position. Explained in further chapters.

Steps to Shift the Frets

The following is a 3 step technique to convert Shuddha swaras to komal swaras by shifting the frets upward on the fingerboard:

Step 1 - Stand the sitar on the floor on the gourd.

Step 2 - Push the fret up using thumb and fingers; first left then right side.

Step 3 - Push the fret to the accurate distance and make it equal on both sides.

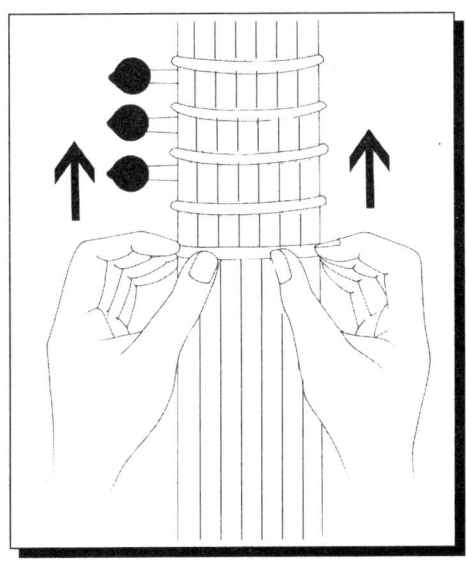

Playing Basic Swaras

Production of basic notes *(Swaras)* on sitar :

The natural notes are played on every octave of a Sitar. There are 7 shuddha swaras, 4 komal and 1 tivra swar and one **Sa** note of the next octave completes the octave.

The left hand index finger is used to press the string right below the desired string to produce the note fixed to that fret. The actual position of fret pressing should be between frets.

Lets learn to play all the 12 notes of the octave.

1. **Sa:** The first note is Sa. Sa is produced when you press the 1st finger of the left hand on **fret no. 7** and using the Da bol played by the right hand stroke.

2. **Re:** The second note is Re. Re is produced when you press the 1st finger of the left hand on **fret no. 8** using the Da bol played by the right hand stroke.

3. **Ga:** The third note is Ga. Ga is produced when you press the 1st finger of the left hand on **fret no. 10** using the Da bol played by the right hand stroke.

4. **Ma:** The fourth note is Ma. Ma is produced when you press the 1st finger of the left hand on **fret No. 11** using the Da bol played by the right hand stroke.

5. **Pa:** The fifth note is Pa. Pa is produced when you press the 1st finger of the left hand on **fret no. 13** using the Da bol played by the right hand stroke.

6. **Dha:** The sixth note is Dha. Dha is produced when you press the 1st finger of the left hand on **fret no. 14** using the Da bol played by the right hand stroke.

7. **Ni:** The seventh note is Ni. Ni is produced when you press the 1st finger of the left hand on **fret no. 16** using the Da bol played by the right hand stroke.

8. **Sa:** The eighth & last note of the octave is Sa of the upper octave. Sa is produced when you press the 2nd *finger* of the left hand on **fret no. 17** using the Da bol played by the right hand stroke.

Komal Swar

The 4 komal swaras are Re, Ga, Dha, Ni.

Every note has a specific fret on the fingerboard of the sitar. There are only two komal swaras, Re & Dha that are not played on the frets. These two komal swaras are produced either by using the Meend* technique or the other by shifting the fret of the same sound half way up, to make them komal or Shuddha.

Komal Re: To position komal Re we have to shift the fret no.8 of shuddha Re upwards towards fret no.7. Another way of producing komal Re is by meend technique, where the played string is pulled down halfway on the 7th fret position to sound komal Re, right after striking 'Da' bol.

Komal Ga is played on the Sitar's fingerboard which is fret no.9. It is not a movable fret. Komal Ga can also be produced by the meend technique by pulling the string down halfway on fret no.8 to sound komal Ga.

Komal Dha: To position komal Dha, we have to shift fret no.13 of shuddha Dha halfway upwards to fret no.12. Playing komal Dha using meend technique; the string is pulled down halfway from the 12th fret position to sound komal Dha, right after striking it.

Komal Ni is played on the fingerboard which is on fret no.15. Komal Ni can also be produced using the meend technique by pulling the string down halfway on fret no.14 to sound komal Ni.

Tivra Swar

Tivra Ma : Tivra Ma of the middle octave is found on fret no.12 on the fingerboard. To Play it by meend technique pull the string down halfway on fret no.11 to sound Tivra Ma.

Important Techniques implied in sitar Playing

1. Meend
2. Gamak
3. Murki
4. Kan
5. Zamzama
6. Krintan
7. Sparsh
8. Toda
9. Taan
10. Jhala

> **Note:** All the bols are produced by pressing the first finger of the left hand except the last bol, that is Sa of the upper octave. It is produced by pressing the 2nd finger of the left hand.

Part- 6
Tuning and Maintenance of a Sitar

Tuning the Sitar

These days musicians use two ways to tune the sitar.

(a) Tuning with the help of a Piano, an Organ or Harmonium: This method is very simple and direct. It is useful for beginners.

(b) Independent tuning: This type of tuning is based on the sound of a string gauge or an orchestra's fixed note.

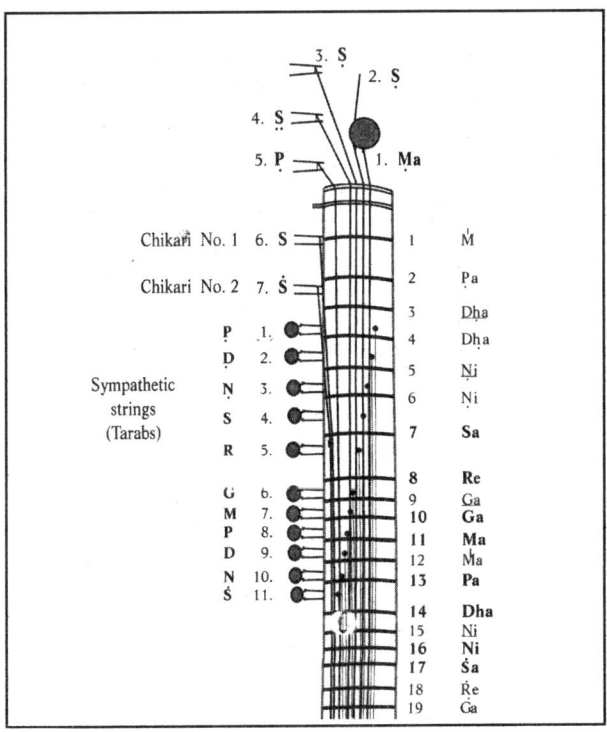

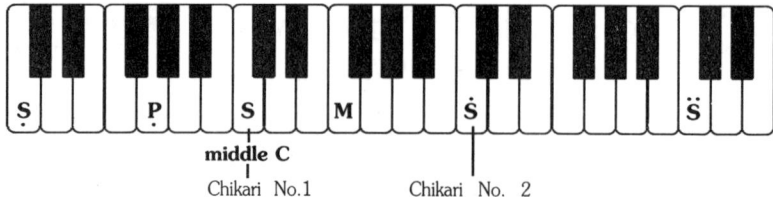

Tuning with the help of a Piano or Harmonium

Tuning the *Jora* (2nd and 3rd strings) with the help of a Harmonium. The 2nd and 3rd strings are both made of bronze and are called the **jora** which means that they are tuned to the same note. These two strings are tuned to the **C note** (Sa) of the lower octave. Both these strings are the basis for tuning the other strings.

1. **STRING NO. 1** is a steel string and is tuned to the **note F** (Ma) of the lower octave.

2. **STRING NO. 4** is a bronze string called the **Kharaj** and is tuned to the **note C** (Sa), two octaves lower from the jora.

3. **STRING NO. 5** also a steel string called the **Pancham or Laraj.** It is tuned to the **note G** (Pa) of the lower octave.

4. **STRING NO. 6** is called the **Chikari** No.1. It is a steel string and is tuned to the **note C** (Sa) of the medium octave.

5. **STRING NO. 7** is also a steel string. It is called the **Chikari** No. 2 and is tuned to the **note C** (Sa) of the upper octave.

Independent Tuning of the Sitar
(with the help of frets)

Jora (String No. 2 & 3) — First of all stretch string No. 2 upto a point that it will neither break nor is too loose. Check the sound of the string with the stroke of the *mizrab*. It will be the **note C** (Sa) of the lower octave. Adjust string No.3 to the sound of string No. 2. Both these strings are called the *Jora*, which is the basic note for tuning the other strings.

String No. 1

It is tuned to the **note F** (Ma) of the lower octave in relation to the sound of string No. 2, (the Jora) when striking it with the *mizrab*, press it on fret No. 5.

String No. 4

This string is tuned to the **note C** (Sa) two octaves lower; i.e. a lower sound produced as compared to the *Jora* (the 2nd & 3rd Strings).

String No. 5

This string is tuned to the **note G** (Pa) of the lower octave, according to the sound obtained from string No.1 when striking it with the *mizrab,* press it on fret No.2.

String No. 6 (Chikari No.1)

This String is tuned to the **note C** (Sa) of the medium octave, according to the sound played on string No.1 pressing it on fret No.7.

String No. 7 (Chikari No.2)

This string is tuned to the **note C** (Sa) of the upper octave, according to the sound played on string no.1 pressing it on fret No.17.

Tuning Chart with the Help of Piano or Harmonium

String No.	String Metal	Gauge	Tuned to Note		Octave
			Indian Swaras	Western Note	
1.	Steel	30	Ṃ	F	Lower
2.	Bronze	27 or 28	Ṣ	C	Lower
3.	Bronze	27 or 28	Ṣ	C	Lower
4.	Steel	30 or 32	Ṗ	G	Lower
5.	Bronze	21 or 26	S̤	C	Double lower
6.	Steel (Chikari No.1)	33 or 34	S	C	Medium
7.	Steel (Chikari No.2)	33 or 34	Ṡ	C	Upper

Tuning Chart with the Help of Frets

String No.	String No. To be Tuned tuned on	Fret No. To be pressed	Indian Swaras	Western Note	Octave
1	1 2	5	Ṃ	F	Lower
2	2 + 3 Self	—	Ṣ	C	Lower
4	4 Help of Jora Sound	—	Ṣ	C	Double Lower
5	5 —	2	Ṗ	G	Lower
6	6 1	7	S	C	Medium
7	7 1	17	Ṡ	C	Upper

Tuning of Sympathetic Strings (Tarabs)

The sympathetic strings are 11 or 13 in number and all are made of Steel. They are fixed under the frets but on top of the finger board. They are not struck by the *mizrab* but when the player strikes the *mizrab* on the upper main strings which produces the sound, this sound vibrates the sympathetic strings which automatically produces sounds. These sympathetic strings are tuned on the basic notes of the **Thaats**, which the players play their **gats** in any of the **ragas**.

Tuning Chart of Sympathetic Strings

With the help of Piano or Harmonium				With the help of frets pressed on string No. 1 Sound Produced By String				
String No.	Swara	Western Note	Octave	String No.	Fret Nos.	Swara	Western Note	Octave
1	P̣	G	Lower	1	2	P̣	G	Lower
2	Ḍ	A	"	2	4	Ḍ	A	"
3	Ṇ	B	"	3	6	Ṇ	B	"
4	S	C	Medium	4	7	S	C	Medium
5	R	D	"	5	8	R	D	"
6	G	E	"	6	10	G	E	"
7	M	F	"	7	11	M	F	"
8	P	G	"	8	13	P	G.	"
9	D	A	"	9	14	D	A	"
10	N	B	"	10	16	N	B	"
11	Ṡ	C	Upper	11	17	Ṡ	C	Upper

(All Strings are steel strings with gauges of 33 or 34)

(Gauges and Sitar strings are explained before)

Repairs & Maintenance of a Sitar

When repairing the Sitar the following can be done easily by the player himself to keep the instrument in good working condition :

(i) Replacing string.

(ii) Tightening the frets.

(iii) Polishing the top of the Bridge for a clear sound of the strings.

Replacing the Upper Strings

First of all make a hook of the string and place it on the end pin. Pass the other end of the string over the bridge and make a hook at one end of the string and place it on the end pin as above, then passing the second end over the bridge and ivory nail, tie it to the tuning peg holes.

Replacing the Sympathetic Strings

Make a hook at one end of the string and place it on the end pin. Now thread it under the large bridge, over the small bridge. After removing the peg let it feed through the proper hole on the finger board and then take it out with the help of a wire hook and after that fit it to the peg. Adjust the peg at the proper place.

Tightening the Frets

First of all place the fret on the finger board, take a nylon thread and prepare a hook to make a knot. Press it with the left hand thumb on the finger board where one end of the fret is placed. Then making two or three rounds of the nylon thread through the cuttings of the fret, tie it firmly to the hook under the thumb. Tie a knot on the side of the pegs.

Polishing the Top of the Bridge

It is often seen that with constant playing, there are some kind of scratches made on top of the bridge. These scratches make the instrument dull. Hence it requires polishing. To do this loosen the strings and clean the surface of the bridge with a zero number sand paper or file.

Maintenance of the Sitar

(1) The instrument must be protected from extreme weather conditions.

(2) When not in use the upper strings must be loosen to one note lower.

(3) If it is to be kept in a corner, place it in a plastic or cotton cover in a standing position with the front facing the wall.

(4) Keeping the Sitar safe, a wooden box duly lined with cotton sheet or velvet cloth may be used, to protect it from weather changes.

(5) When transporting the instrument from place to place without a box, hold it firmly between the right arm and the side of the chest, holding the finger board with the right hand. Keep the gourd backward to protect it from getting hit.

Tips for Buying a Sitar

When it comes to buying a sitar we often get puzzled and think what to do and what not. There are a number of variety and design of sitars available in the market. Any ordinary buyer will be confused to see the available designs in the market and may be deceived by the shop keeper with an inferior quality in the price of a superior one. Therefore the following points should be kept in mind when purchasing a sitar.

TIP 1. Normally a new buyer is attracted to the beauty of a sitar but remember that it is the sound quality and not the appearance that is important. A buyer should note the tonal quality of a sitar. The sound must be round and sweet.

TIP 2. The quality of wood used in the sitar is very important. A Sitar with seasoned wood is normally preferred because this type of wood is resistant against weather conditions and lasts longer.

TIP 3. The materials used in the sitar should be of good quality. Such as the frets of a sitar should be made up of a good alloy that does not get rusted. The beads and mankas should be made of ivory for longer life.

TIP 4. Price is another aspect to be kept in mind. Initially a cheaper sitar will do because there is danger of wear and tear in a new hand. Later on when one has mastered the art a new and better quality may be purchased.

Notes

PANKAJ PUBLICATIONS
Suggested Readings on Strings Instruments

Learn to Play on Sitar

ISBN: 81-87155-14-0

A Best-seller book of the popular 'Learn to Play series', talks about Learning the worlds' favorite instrument in detail. Pictorial details of handling, postures and tuning the instrument for the comfort of every learner. A sure pick for the advance learners.

Sitar - Learn & Play

A Detail book on Sitar Learning with colored pictures explaining positions, postures and playing. The book is available in both HINDI & ENGLISH language. A series of exercises are given for practicing advance techniques of sitar playing. Comes along with an audio C.D. Explaining sounds of sitar.

PANKAJ PUBLICATIONS

- Presents -
Practice books for music Learners
SELECTED HINDI SONGS
WITH NOTATIONS & CHORDS

The series presents the songbooks of a collection of songs for early musicians to practice. The notations with the songs let learners practice to play the songs on Indian Notation System and on chords. The series has collection of songs in Hindi, as well as their romanized version for easy readability for English speaking people.

PANKAJ PUBLICATIONS

Learn to Play on... Series

Book Name	ISBN
Learn to play on Tabla Vol-1	81-87155-00-0
Learn to play on Tabla Vol-2	81-87155-01-9
Learn to play on Harmonium	81-87155-22-1
Learn to play on Flute	81-87155-33-7
Learn to play on Sitar	81-87155-14-0
Learn to play on Violin	81-87155-46-9
Learn to play on Veena	81-87155-47-7
Learn to play on Guitar	81-87155-15-9
Learn to play on Mouth Organ	81-87155-03-5
Learn to play on Bongo-Congo	81-87155-68-X
Guitar Chords	81-87155-16-7
Indian Dances for Beginners	81-87155-02-7
MIND OVER FINGERS	81-87155-80-9
Distinction! in Music Theory Exam	81-87155-94-9

For Information or to Order,

Please visit our website: **www.pankajmusic.com**
or Email us at: contact@pankajmusic.com
or simply write to: **Pankaj Publications, 3, Regal Building, Sansad Marg, New Delhi - 1100 01.**